Amazing Snakes

Written by Mary-Anne Creasy

Flying Start
to Literacy®

Contents

Introduction

Snakes are amazing hunters.

They have many different ways to catch, kill and eat their food. They are able to grab their food very quickly.

Chapter 1

Catching food

Snakes catch their food in different ways.

Using sight

Some snakes have very good sight, which helps when they hunt.

A king cobra can see an animal nearly 100 metres away. This helps it to find animals for food.

king cobra

Using hearing

Snakes do not have ears on the outside
of their bodies, but snakes can hear.
They can feel the vibrations of sound.

Snakes use their sense of hearing
to find animals to eat.

Sensing heat

Some snakes have heat-sensing organs on their bodies that can "feel" the heat of animals nearby.

This helps them to catch animals they cannot see. The heat-sensing organs also help them to hunt in the dark.

A python has heat-sensing organs along its mouth.

A rattlesnake has a heat-sensing organ under its eye.

Scientists have done experiments with rattlesnakes to find out about their heat-sensing organs. In these experiments, blindfolded rattlesnakes were able to catch running rats.

Trapping animals

Some snakes catch food by staying very still and waiting for animals to come close. The snakes can quickly grab the animals.

Snakes that catch food in this way are usually the same colour as the places where they live. This makes it hard for other animals to see them.

rattlesnake

death adder

The death adder lies still and wiggles its tail, which looks like a worm. The tail looks like food to birds and mice. When they come close to its tail, the death adder catches them.

Chapter 2

Killing food

Snakes kill the animals they catch.
They kill them in different ways.

Squeezing

Some snakes kill their food by wrapping their bodies around the animal and squeezing it hard. This stops the animal from breathing and kills it. When the animal stops moving, the snake can swallow it.

Poison

Some snakes kill their food with poison called venom.

Poisonous snakes have sharp, hollow teeth called fangs. When a poisonous snake bites an animal, the venom flows out of its fangs and into the animal.

The poison kills the animal. Then the snake can eat it.

A gaboon viper has fangs that are so long they can fold back into its mouth.

Chapter 3

Eating food

Snakes cannot chew their food or rip it into small pieces, so they must swallow their food in one piece.

Snakes have amazing jaws that can stretch wide open. This allows them to swallow food much thicker than their heads and bodies.

Most snakes eat about once every week. Some eat only once a month.

18

Many snakes have teeth that point backwards into their mouths. They use these teeth to pull themselves over the animals they eat. It can take these snakes a long time to swallow an animal.

Conclusion

Snakes are amazing hunters. They hunt in many different ways.

Snakes use their senses to catch their food.

They have different ways of killing and eating their food.

Amazing hunters

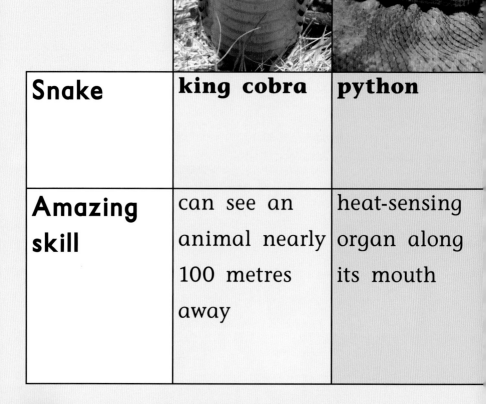

Snake	**king cobra**	**python**
Amazing skill	can see an animal nearly 100 metres away	heat-sensing organ along its mouth

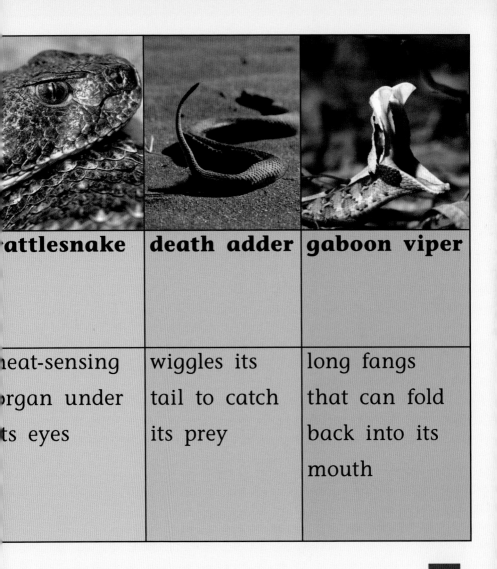

rattlesnake	death adder	gaboon viper
heat-sensing organ under its eyes	wiggles its tail to catch its prey	long fangs that can fold back into its mouth

Index